Posada: Offerings of Witness and Refuge

Sundress Publications • Knoxville, TN

ISBN: 978-1-939675-42-2
Library of Congress: 2016950619
Published by Sundress Publications
www.sundresspublications.com

Editor: Erin Elizabeth Smith
Editorial Assistant: Jane Huffman

Special thanks to Montreaux Rotholtz.

Colophon: This book is set in Latin Modern Roman.

Cover Image: Erika Monique Medrano Bermejo

Cover Design: Kristen Ton

Book Design: Erin Elizabeth Smith

Posada: Offerings of Witness and Refuge

Xochitl-Julisa Bermejo

ACKNOWLEDGEMENTS

Grateful acknowledgment is made to the editors of the following publications where these poems, or earlier versions, first appeared:

The Acentos Reivew: I Didn't Know I could Love the Desert, Nobody Wanted a Mountain to Hate Him, Paper Birds

The American Poetry Review: La Perrera of Chavez Ravine

Angel's Flight Literary West: Posada, Standing Before Zorba the Great, The Story of the Stolen Metate

The Best American Poetry blog: Our Lady of the Water Gallons

Cactus Heart: For Sensitive Skin

Calaveras Fronteras (Mouthfeel Press): Gabrielito's Crab

CALYX: Frida's Monkey Nurse

Coiled Serpent: Poets Arising from the Cultural Quakes and Shifts of Los Angeles (Tia Chucha Press): The Boys of Summer, Ode to Pan Dulce

Crazyhorse: Mediation for the Lost and Found

Cultural Weekly: The Ascension of Josseline, Our Lady of the Water Gallons

Latinopia: Our Lady of the Water Gallons (video)

The Los Angeles Review: Mud-caked, Photograph of a Secret, to chew   empty spaces

Lumen Magazine: Cascarones

Malpais Review: Blue Bride, Ladder to the Moon

Mujeres de Maiz: Letter from the Desert

Poets Responding to SB 1070, *La Bloga* Online Floricanto: The Boys of summer, Search and Recovery

Political Punch (Sundress Publications): Meditation for the Lost and Found, Our Lady of the Water Gallons, Ventana

Tahoma Literary Review: Upon Celebrating America's Birthday

The Museum of All Things Awesome and that Go Boom (Upper Rubber Boot): Photograph of a Secret

"Things to Know for Comapañer@s" was first published as a DIY poem-map designed and printed by Ashaki M. Jackson and sold to raised funds for No More Deaths.

TABLE OF CONTENTS

Dedicated to my grandmother, Ubalda D. Bermejo (1921—2013).
She was my L.A. and my safe place.

Solano Says Goodbye

After Sandra Cisneros

I moved to Solano Canyon to feel close to history, to coax Chavez Ravine ghosts from darkness, to ask hills to speak. By day, I explored trails and encountered discarded mattresses, old shoes, water bottles, loose newspaper pages: signs that ghosts were not ghosts at all. At dusk, the canyon swelled with coyote ballads and cactus lessons, but at night, lost objects and the left-behind-people they belonged to danced around my bed. Night air was strange with spirits. Always a curious girl willing to see a path past its bend, I'm ready now to turn around, pack up and find a place more like home. I leave this for those who want to find home too, but can't.

PART I

The Story of the Stolen Metate

When my grandparents moved to the little house on Fairmont Avenue their belongings were scattered about the lawn as children of all sizes ran up and down red stoop steps to carry items inside one by one. In the commotion, a faceless neighbor or passerby lifted my grandmother's black lava metate and mano, and the tools were never seen again.

I wonder if my father's shoulders felt their weight lifted when the burglar picked the items from the yard. As eldest son, it was surely his job to carry the stone kitchen appliance along with the molcajete, my grandmother's only valuables, from Mexico.

I imagine him walking hunched back with the tools slung over a shoulder, black legs protruding from a rainbow sarape. He leads a baby brother by the hand, while my grandmother follows close behind swaddling an ill daughter and calling to a wild, travieso second son to hurry up.

I see them, five in all, on a crowded bus traveling a dusty road north to meet my grandfather in Tijuana. He was in charge of handling the papers. My father, of holding them tight—his siblings and his hand-carved inheritance.

I didn't hear the story of the stolen metate until after my grandmother's death. Her seven children gathered in the little Fairmount house to organize paperwork, divvy up items, and share stories. My father found his original green card and gifted it to me.

With his black and white adolescent face between fingers I asked, "Who carried the metate and molcajete from Teocaltiche?"

"I don't remember," he said, but it had to be him.

Maybe remembering hurts dusty shoulders, maybe they miss the weight of home too much. Maybe my grandmother's hands missed turning the mano to grind down the corn for tortillas. When I picture her now, I only see hands folded over the kitchen table kneading with worry. Maybe they remembered the question of how to feed the children.

If I could ask her, I imagine she'd say hands are never empty when folded in prayer.

Cascarones

Chavez Ravine, 1949, Don Normark

I

The boy wears a reindeer sweater,
but it's not Christmas.
That's not snow spilling,
but white flakes falling
over the tops of heads
in celebration of Easter.
Cáscaras are carefully
tapped and emptied
by mothers cooking breakfast,
dried and collected
on windowsills over months,
and filled with the promise of smiles
for boys wearing moth-eaten
reindeer sweaters in spring.
Beneath the fresh crack of a cascarón,
all worry breaks to pieces.

II

My great-grandparents
with white hair and chiseled smiles

walk arm in arm before a church.
Andrés wears a thick cardigan,
fat charcoal buttons closed at the neck
and opened above the waist.
Placida wears a black rebozo
over the crown of her head
and her own dark cardigan over a long skirt.
I'm told this is their 50th anniversary.
This is a black and white photo
from Teocaltiche, Mexico.
A black and white photo that lies in a tall stack
of photos waiting to be sorted
by my grandmother's children gathered
in her Boyle Heights home.
Andrés and Placida are long gone.
My grandmother is gone now too.
I want to ask my aunt for this photo
of an old couple frozen before a church
getting rained on by white bits like snow,
but I don't because we are fragile
and in danger of going to pieces.

III

"Did you know it's a Mexican thing?"
"Huh?"
"Confetti eggs. Did you know?"

my cousin asked as she nibbled
on one of my mother's falltime pumpkin
and oatmeal cookies in our kitchen.
She lifted a stockinged foot to the hem
of her polyester skirt looking like a ballerina.
I blushed at the metal-stapled hem of my skirt
scratching at a chubby knee.
"I always thought all kids had confetti eggs,
but they don't."
"Really?" I said thinking of Easter picnics
and tiny bits of colored paper caught
in my curly hair, tiny bits
I could only get out with water and shampoo.
She didn't know about that
with wavy chocolate hair that swayed
about her slender shoulders.
"You grow up thinking all kids
have what you have," she said,
and I thought about her beauty
and how any time we played truth or dare,
all the boys picked dare in the hopes of kissing her,
but never about her absent dad,
or that she spent afternoons at our house
so her mom wouldn't worry while she worked.
All this fell from my 13 year-old mind like confetti,
and only now do I begin to gather the pieces.

Good for Keeping Hold-me-downs Up

Chavez Ravine, 1949, Don Normark

Suspenders: two supporting straps
drawn over shoulders
fastened to trousers

Suspension: the state of a substance
when its particles are mixed with but will not dissolve;

L.A. TIMES, April 2, 2011: Giants Fan Beaten
at Dodger Stadium in Coma

: a form of punishment;

ESPN, May 8, 2009: Manny Ramirez is Banished
for 50 Games

Suspect: to imagine to exist;
baseball heroes and superstars

: to imagine to be guilty;
L.A. homeboys in long shorts
and oversized Dodger jerseys

Suspicion: the act of believing someone is undesirable;

Zoot Suit riots at Sleepy Lagoon
six years before Chavez Ravine, 1949

: a barely detectable amount

Suspend: to harness to some elevated point
without support from below

like a cement foundation

                    or a home

: to bar from privilege

Suspense: state of waiting;
the boy in striped suspenders

Upon Celebrating America's Birthday

In the morning, I explore the yellow hills
of Chavez Ravine and collect trinkets for my desk:
a hawk feather, a sun-bleached snail shell,
a rusted nail sitting within the brick base
ruins of a house. I imagine great-aunt Susana
collecting herbs from the hills hugging Teocaltiche.
In the afternoon, Uncle Manny recalls remedies
she concocted and the tiny quail eggs she fried
for breakfast with handmade tortillas the shape of boats.
My finicky father never ate from her table,
but Uncle Manny has had too many Budweisers
and is spilling memories of his favorite tía this 4th of July.
"She used to put me on her shoulders and carry me
across the river," he says dreamily. This was before L.A.,
hair products, Ford cars, and the church youth group
where he met my aunt, and my dad met my mother.
By dark, tears dig into the creases of his face
like a stone creek. He hushes only to watch my cousins
launch bottle rockets from the street. Smoke tails up
and sparks shoot out over our heads. Colors flash bright
and disappear into the air like my uncle's sobriety,
like Tía Susana, like the houses of Chavez Ravine.

Sunday Morning

The clang of church bells rise over Solano Canyon
drawing believers to this hidden green piece
in the city. Heads bow for those left to gunshots and fires
cracking elsewhere. Here horns and hawk cries crease
the blue air. Bronze and candle-lit saints keep
hillside vigils over offerings and prayers for peace
rising like the clang of church bells over Solano Canyon.

Photograph of a Secret

The Altiplano and Bolivia's New Order, George Steinmetz

The first man tells the second a secret.
A secret that is sinful and burning red
like the walls of their South American bar.
A decorated general framed above listens in.
Two tall beers grow warm from heated words.
It is serious. The harvest is dead,
and my family may lose the land.
It is worse. Your daughter has been ruined
by the town mechanic. Less than that.
Compadre, you have a moco in your nose.
Pick it out before the picture is taken.
No, it is a gripe. Why must these güeros
always take photos of us?
The first man tries to cover his face
while his friend hides behind closed eyes.
No, his friend is asleep and has not heard
a word. Actually, they are not friends at all,
but mortal enemies. The first man whispers,
just wait until I have you alone. I will
slash your throat and bleed you out
like the pig you are. The second man stole
the first man's farm animals. He stole his farm.
He stole his wife. No, it's the other way.

The first man raped the second's daughter,
but the truth burns his ear so bad
all he can do is nod. All he can do is cry.
He cries into his warm beer.
No, they are brothers. Long lost
and sharing their first drink since boyhood.
Since the revolution split them in two.
They are one again.
The first man whispers into the second's ear,
I love you, brother. They must whisper
because they are in a bar with red walls,
and the decorated General is listening in.

Standing before Zorba the Great

Pope of Broadway, Eloy Torrez

I

His arms are open
like my tata's, like a great
big grandfather, and I am so small.

Traffic rolls behind me:
honks, revs, the hydraulic hisses
from bus doors.

Sour smell creeps up my nose.
Tires screech. I jerk my head back
expecting an invading car,

but I am safe
in Zorba's— Anthony's—
Tata's embrace.

II

Zorba is dancing, but he winces.
His shoes need shining,
scuffed by long buffed graffiti,

covered by buffed graffiti.
I want to shine them
the way my father taught me.
I think of my father's cowboy boots:
gray snake skin, peach suede,
brown leather. At night
he came home weathered,
and I charged in to own
my cowboy boot duty.
Two hands clutching a wooden heel,
sitting on the ground, leveraging
feet against carpet, I yanked
till a tired foot angled loose,
and my father, grinning and free.

III

King Kong Quinn rises from concrete,
arms engulfing a building,
but his head is cocked to one side,
eyes are shut, lips open.

They would say, "Oh, him?
That's Mexican Quinn," and I knew
he shone brilliant like polished silver moons,
like undiscovered precious metal.

Metallic and mortar Quinn listens
to a Salvadoreña mother and her American hija's
singsong chatter, to the near silent clink
of change in a fallen man's open hand,

to a pastor's pleading preaching
from an abandoned movie house pulpit.
Holy Padre Quinn invites
a forgotten city to speak.

The Hills of East L.A. Are Home

"I remembered something. I remembered
we used to go to a hill in L.A. to cut nopales
with your grandmother and your Tía Pepa."

My aunt called me in the middle of the day
not so long ago with this piece of family history.
"Do you remember what hill?" I asked

half being polite and half curious to dig for more.
"No, but your dad used to drive us.
Maybe he knows." We are quiet on the line.

I am sitting on my bed in Solano Canyon
watching the neighborhood below my window
move slow in the crack of green hills.

"Anything else?" I ask. "No. I remembered,
and I guess I wanted you to know." She's proud
I write poems and like to listen to old stories.

The hills rise over the houses and traffic of the city
like memories gently rising from my aunt's mind
as she sits in a one bedroom condo in Mesa, Arizona.

She doesn't live in L.A. anymore, but the city
doesn't leave her. The flat grid of her new residence
makes her dreamy for hills and cactus pads like hearts,

and for a brother who drove sisters, aunt and mother
to Montecito Heights on Sunday afternoons,
so they could have something like home for dinner.

My Mother's History, or Pieces I've Gathered so Far

I imagine the moment my mother crossed
the border that she didn't cross
with her feet because she was only a baby.
I picture her swaddled in her mother's arms
in a crisp, white blanket and a white bonnet
with a sweet eyelet trim hanging just above her eyes.
I decide it was a gray Sunday morning
in fall because all her history is cloudy.
Two Christmases ago she learned her parents cited
"shopping and sightseeing" as reasons for the trip
on found legal documents. I wonder how
it felt to find her first lie wasn't her own.

One Sunday breakfast at Norm's Diner
the host asked Dad in Spanish,
"Where are you from?" He answered, *"Jalisco,"*
and they both beamed, very proud of themselves.
"And you?" the host asked Mom.
His Tres Flores-combed hair and pencil mustache
made him look important to me, and I jumped
from the booth, "She was born in Tijuana!"
But the man's mustache kinked
before he turned on his heels and walked away.
"Why did he stop smiling, Mommy?"
"Because he thinks Tijuana is bad," she said.

31

All my life, I've heard the story of how her father
would take her little sister and brothers to Tijuana,
but she was never allowed to go. I picture her
a little girl, elbows at a window, waving goodbye
to her family driving away down a tree-lined street.
The TV is on in the background and plays
Father Knows Best. Somewhere else in the house
her mother resents being left behind too.
After a long while, she turns back to the TV
and watches the father give advice, the father
hug and kiss each of his children. "I used to think,"
she'd tell me, "he must not be my dad."

I ask now and again when she knew the truth.
Sometimes she is 12, others 14. "When my parents
said we were going to Tijuana to find my birth certificate."
They only managed to unearth a baptismal one.
Everything is in pieces like shards of ancient pottery.
I see now, she was never gifted the story of her birth,
never wished happy birthday at a specific time of day,
never doted over with funny stories of a father
who splurged on three tiny purses the day she was born.
History is haunted by two ugly and unspoken words:
illegitimate and illegal. "I hope I'm better," she often said.
"All I've wanted was to be a better mother than mine."

At Mark Keppel High School she was placed
in remedial classes because it was the sixties
and she was a wetback. No one ever taught her
proper English or Spanish. She handed me this shard
when I was about to go into high school,
and I begged her to take me out of my private school.
By then it was the nineties, but she wise enough
to not see a difference. "I promised myself
when I had kids they would never go to public."
On this point she was clear, but she tends to talk
in circles. I guess that's a consequence
of growing up without a language or a land.

In her high school days, her father would vanish
below the border for weeks at a time. There he wore
fine, tailored suits he made himself and answered to
"Don Prudencio." I think being revered is a drug
because he left his wife and children behind
in a rented L.A. house with no electricity.
A handsome, widowed neighbor at times ran
a power cord from his house to theirs for light.
"I remember he had kids too, and I wanted him
to marry my mom," Aunt Lala laughed, sharing a story
I'd never heard. Mom huffed, "I don't remember."
It must be easier sometimes to live in the dark.

She taught herself to escape into black and white TV
and silver movies. Taught herself to survive
on predictable stories with beautifully tailored men,
feisty women, and easy endings. "I always can tell
what's going to happen," she says as a gripe,
but clearly revels in the knowing. "I used to know
all the classics," she still brags when I find her
jaw-slacked, eyes blank before the TV on hot afternoons.
It's not surprising my second name "Julisa"
was chosen for her favorite Mexican actress,
but we are surprised to find her second name "Nora"
was taken at months old. She never even knew.

"Aunt Elena," a cousin called to her from across a table
muddied with hojas, masa and rellenos.
Tamale Day was here and the house stuffed with family.
They came to make Mom's recipes, drink Dad's alcohol
and laugh. It's a tradition she started 30 years earlier.
"Aunt Elena," she said again louder to catch her attention.
"Did you know you have a middle name?"
"No," Mom shrugged and dug strong hands into masa.
"How do you know?" I asked, receiving this newest piece.
"It's on a border document I found at ancestry.com."
Before I could reply she added, "Isn't that funny?"
But I could see my mother's eyes turning to glass.

Posada

A young girl sings *Noche de Paz*
through a silent East L.A. night.
From my Grandmother's stoop, I watch
families weave winter streets by candlelight.
Inside, my grandmother sets knitting needles down
to listen. We have found our shelter tonight
as a young girl sings *Noche de Paz*.

La Posada de Los Angeles

Una muchacha canta *Noche de Paz*
en las calles del barrio. Desde la entrada
de la casa de mi abuela, yo observo
familias desfilando bajo la luz de las velas.
Adentro, mi abuela descansa sus manos del tejido
y escucha la canción. En el refugio de la casa,
encontramos nuestra noche de paz.

PART II

Ladder to the Moon

Ladder to the Moon, Georgia O'Keeffe

At Ghost Ranch, O'Keeffe's
sprite spirit rises

like the waif of moon
over Perdenal's inky, cut top.

It's an aquamarine night
when I catch her climb wooden rails

to the sky. Her frail arms
evoke twigs, but her eyes

ignite like the stars.
I want her to invite me up,

but she doesn't.
I want her to teach me how,

but she won't.
I kick red rocks across the land

and keep a look out
for my own blond ladder to blaze.

Blue Bride

Bride and Groom, Ken Twitchell

She is blue.
Eyes and fingers blue.
Satin and lace blue.
Why so blue?
Psychedelic ribbon hair curls up
like algae blue,
like seaweed wrapping
around forgotten body blue.
It calls her down.
Trapped in blue.

She is my mother.
She is powder blue-ruffled
1971-pregnant in beaded tulle.
A weathered mermaid,
water, weight and shame
crack a left mollusk eye.

She will birth a sea monster
from her wet womb.
Not monster, but seahorse,
light and dancing.
Not seahorse, but walrus,

lard rolls protecting
from the chill.
Better, a purple octopus.

I will transform my brother
into a fire-orange crab side-stepping
dark water beginnings,
but my mother,
she has always been sinking,
lips sealed, unable to smile.
Lost in blue.

Frida's Monkey Nurse

Self-Portrait with Thorn Necklace and Hummingbird, Frida Kahlo

I crafted the necklace. I twisted
the thorns and browned-vines
into patterns and paths
fit to drape her frame. I knotted
the midnight raven to her nape.

My small black fingers bled
red drips. Don't think they didn't.
But she is a demanding woman-child.
I know. I nursed her from birth.
She never told you that, did she?

When she was a girl, I was stationed
to straighten her skirt as she crawled
back and forth through her door in glass.
Like Alice, she was too eager
to jump through the rabbit hole.

She never cared where it spit her out:
in the courtyard, beneath
the kitchen table, tossing
down the stairs. I was there,
I was everywhere. Guarding, waiting

to catch her, to fix her. She never
not needed fixing. I was on the bus too,
weaving brown braids
into ribbons and butterflies,
the way she insisted, when her body

unraveled: backbone shattering
into gold dust. And I
was called on to nurse her again.
Washed her body, washed
her brushes, brushed her hair.

And I held up the mirror: the glass door
to her other world. I was everywhere.
And now, I sit at her side
braiding thorns instead of ribbons.
She prefers it. Fingers bleed,

but what can I do? I knit
ravens and roots, vines and veins.
I tie her to this world never knowing
where the other will spit her out, never knowing
when it will finally swallow her whole.

Gabrielito's Crab

His eyes are so deep
I want to dip toes in
and find the fountain
of his youthfulness,
the pond where he fishes
his imagination from
like the silvery cod
he pretends to catch.
No, it's not a fish,
but the red crab we cross
on a beach path turned
over and hollowed by
black ants and a hot sun.
I think I hear crackling,
blood baking into shell,
but Gabrielito,
he holds my hand and points,
"I think he's in his dream.
Tía, he is dreaming."
And like the click of a slide,
we are in negative.
The sky is red and the crab blue,
Gabrielito blue, my hand
holding his, blue.
We are characters cast

in the crab's dream.
My forehead sweats worry,
but Gabrielito smiles,
deep water eyes fixing on mine,
and I am back with the living.
Cupping fingers around
brown-rosed cheeks,
I tell him I love him
and fear the day he discovers
cobalt crabs guarding
the cliffs of the afterworld.

This Poem is for Nopales

Those green prickly plants made of arms like roof tiles.
The ones my grandmother cleaned of needles
before chopping and boiling for dinner.
Those tender emerald bites dropped in my belly like a love letter.
Overnight nopales spring and fan across Los Angeles to brag
they are native to this continent. Native like her. Native like me.

I want to cut one paddle off the hill outside my door,
slice the needles with a sharp knife like she showed me,
carve a heart in its center, place a stamp on it,
and send it as a postcard with the word, "Extraño."
But because I can't, I'll nail it to the peach wall in my kitchen
and wait for it to sprout and glow in the night.

This poem is for chin hairs. Those chin hairs that stuck out
black and coarse from the soft skin of her face just like nopal needles.
She was always a nopal faithfully keeping vigil over our family.
Now, she is the nopal kissing the Virgen's feet.

Grandma, in the hospital room, when I kissed the fade of your cheek
to say goodbye, crisscrossing chin hairs caught my attention.
Now, when I look in the mirror and find hairs have bloomed overnight,
I think of roots. I think of you. I hope I can be a nopal woman too.

Ode to Pan Dulce

When I bathe you in the aguas termales of my coffee,
and you happily soak in the heat and steam,

what more can I do but place you on my tongue
and recibirte como un sacrament?

Your warmth radiates from my mouth
lighting the esquinas oscuras of my mind

where I find my tata bien sentada on his corner stool
in the little pistachio kitchen in Boyle Heights.

Ojos brillantes, sugar dusting white stubble, he laughs.
Here his sonrisa grows and cancer never shrivels lips.

Panecito mio, lightweight and delicate in my palm,
pájaro about to fly, I want save you in tissue

like chile picked from the yard already wrinkling.
Like unraveling yarn-end of sueños that tangle on wake,

I throw myself into an embrace with a long dead friend.
I notice his favorite red jacket and think, *Where have you been?*

This is how you are panecito. A perfect holy circle
filling my hungry soul with lost loves that now and again regresan.

You are the warm silence that filled the air between
Grandma leyendo oraciones and me reading poems.

You are Tata's booming laugh. You are the Español swimming
in my mind. You are one single moment, a bite.

Paper Birds

Slathering homemade glue, they make kites from newspaper
and bamboo. "Mira, look, mira. Like this. This is how

we did it in Teocaltiche." A father demonstrates how to
structure the body by bowing a wing, fanning a tail.

The children—Gabriel, Diane, Andrés, Angelica, Ricky,
Micky, Maggie, Erika, Gloria, Abram, and Xochitl—unroll

across a manicured green lawn, front stoop to black gate.
Safely corralled from Fairmont noise, they work for flight with hands.

Whose black and white bird will catch the wind? Whose will crash
and die? "Yours is full of holes. I'll call it Patchy." Ricky baptizes

Maggie's creation, and one by one they each offer their animals
to the sun, beaks first, yarn tails cascading like quetzal feathers.

At Wabash and Evergreen a little girl exits the corner market
—newly bought saladito on her tongue—to discover

hand-crafted parrots reaching over rooftops, clearing the old synagogue
now new Christian. She imagines the houses turning to paper too

and lifting from concrete. Tonight she will dream
her intestine is the string, she the kite. Tonight she will dream.

Mud-caked

Chavez Ravine, 1949, Don Normark

Stone-black eyes spy boys wrestling feet away.
She clutches her war-torn Kewpie-faced bunny
by one tattered ear. This is her bunny, her ally,
her corner of dirt. Backs pressed
to a wood-planked wall, they keep
a dedicated lookout. Her stone eyes aim
left; Bunny's, scratched out, shift right.
Boys can battle for brown-grassed hills,
but they won't snatch Bunny—one mud-caked,
plump-stuffed bunny—from her tight grip.
When she goes in for the night
she will tie Bunny to a pipe with twine:
her bunny, her patch of dirt, her pipe and twine.
Like a horse at a saloon, she will tie Bunny up
before supper, before her mother can say,
"Don't you dare bring that filthy thing in,"
a pointed finger commanding, "¡Basura!"
But Bunny is secured to a pipe with twine
and enjoys two ears clogged with dirt.

August Rose

After Eileen Myles

Today, exploring a poet's novel, I discovered
a girl named Rose. The poet, Eileen, fell in love with Rose.
It was a firsts kind of love. Rose was the first
to share with Eileen her sun, and she, in turn,
was awakened to her own inferno.
That's what roses are like—boastful, burning birth
and alluring, radiant death. Suddenly, I felt a need
to pick Rose from the pages and swaddle her in my arms.
Rose, the perfect name for a baby,
but I just had an IUD inserted into my beautiful cervix
in a sterile room with posters of ballet puppies posing
over my head, and now I can choose
to not be pregnant for the next five years.
By then I will be 37 and my ovaries
morning blooms browning at the tips by noon.
The insertion was days ago, and my velveteen vagina
is open, red and raw. My uterus cramps and squeezes,
and this body doesn't know what it's fighting,
but it wants a break. But wait!
I wanted this poem to be about new love
and the magenta roses he placed at my door
with handwritten notes saying, "Thinking of you."
The roses he snipped from their stems,

the roses I placed in my hair, the pink petals
he scattered over grey sheets, those shriveled petals
I still find under my bed. I wanted Rose to represent what rose up
in us that infernal August, but now I fear
this love will wither too. But maybe that doesn't matter
because from the moment I saw Rose
unfold over a yellowing page, I felt her
wrestling inside my body desperate to be known.

Prayer to St. Anthony of Padua

St. Anthony, six months ago
a blond, long-haired gypsy
in the rolling hills of California
splayed cards in a Celtic Cross.
One by one, swords, drops of blood,
a dagger pierced heart were turned over,
and her face went dark.
"What does it mean?" I asked.
"Can't you see?" With no wink in her eye
she said, "You will never find love."
I can't have that, St. Anthony!
I drove across the southwest
to climb a red vortex at sunrise.
I waited for a 360 world to ignite in light
before I knelt to the rock, picked up three stones,
gripped them to my breast and begged
for those cards to be wrong.
Now I have you hanging upside down
over my desk, candles lit, tower of red stones
making a sad little altar so that I can
request a man, so that I can
have someone to hold, so that I do not die alone.
Ever since I was a child, I've had a habit
of losing precious things.
Once it was my father's gold

and alexandrite ring, like a class ring
without the emblems.
It slipped off my wet finger one afternoon
when I was playing in the park sprinklers.
I still imagine it waiting in green blades,
the cut stone changing colors with the sun
working every angle to be seen.
St. Anthony, I'm ready to be found.
If you help me, I will braid up all my curls,
cut off the mass, and place it as a pillow
below your blood-rushed head. I'll give you
every strand. I'll build you a tower of hair.

The Art of Touch

He touched my naked body,
one fingertip molding lines,
shaping shoulders, as if he the sculptor
and me the sculpture and the muse.

I've always wanted to be her,
desire and beauty, and to hang up
all my impossible hang-ups on a hook
like a hat, keys, the phone.

His electric, super-power touch
on a grey Sunday morning
granted such a wish as he awoke
an elbow, a breast, a neck, cheek, lips.

He fed this new body with licks
from a pulsating tongue, and breathed life
into groggy limbs with a pursed hush
hovering over hungry skin.

But that wasn't the start. The night before—
when he invited me to remove shoes
at the door, nude toes free to drink particles of floor,
tiny yarns of carpet tickling the curve of foot—

is when the touching began.

La Perrera of Chavez Ravine

Chavez Ravine, 1949, Don Normark

La Perrera lived with a handsome man
much younger than her.
Neighbor women gossiped across clotheslines
that she held him with witchcraft.
But it was long, black braids streaked white
that kept him coming to her bed.
At night, she entwined his taut body to her,
braids weaving through limbs,
around iron posts of her bed,
between wooden slats of her shack,
until she, he and everything around became one.

But on August days, when want grew restless,
she commanded black braids like hound dogs,
like hairy henchmen, to sniff him out
of factories or construction sites
and guide him home. Once, he was in an orchard
as far out as Oxnard with arms full of oranges
when braids hunted him down.
Bright orbs dropped to the fertile soil,
and off he was led back to her bosom, to her lips,
to her hips, bed and shack. But he never minded
when he found himself wrapped in her.

PART III

Things to Know for Compañer@s

A No More Deaths Volunteer Guide

Did you know?

A baby rattlesnake's venom is more lethal because it knows no control. Woolly, mammoth tarantulas inch across the road at dusk—not down it. Why did the tarantula cross the road? To eat the chicken.

Did you know?

Everything in the desert is as alert as a needle and just as sharp. It is possible to comically sit on a cactus, though you probably won't laugh. Crimson scratches and emerald bruises will be your medals.

Did you know?

When patrolling trails, you may encounter a mountain lion. If so, gather together, stand tall and wave your arms. When encountering lightning, spread out and crouch close to the ground. Do not confuse the two.

Did you know?

Tu Español puede ayudar a salvar una vida. *Compañero* is Spanish for we are in this shit together. Do not be afraid to speak Spanish.

Did you know?

When you don't have a mirror, you can't care what you look like. When you can't remember what a shower feels like, dirt and sweat cake your clothes, and you want to forget everything sticking to your soul, you won't be too shy to skinny dip.

Did you know?

When barrel cacti become tombstones and their yellow starburst blooms offerings for the dead, you won't be too cool to belt Katy Perry songs.

Did you know?

Orange poppies grow on slopes, oak trees in creeks, and washes are not fixed cement slabs. A mile in the city is nothing like a mile in the desert, and as-the-crow-flies is an optical illusion to hikers relying on hand-held, pixilated GPS.

Did you know?

There will be a moment when you fantasize crashing
water gallons down on the rocks, throwing off your
pack, collapsing on the trail and quitting. This is
when you are to stop and rest. There are people in
the desert who are never allowed rest.

Did you know?

One gallon of water weighs 8.35 pounds. To stay hydrated, a person should drink 1-2 gallons a day. Migrants carry a single oil-black gallon in calloused hands for a three-or-more day trip. Why is it black? So as not to glow.

Did you know?

Migrants are hurried over trails at night and without light. Their blisters are caused by continuous friction, muscle cramping by dehydration, vomiting by drinking bacteria ridden cow pond water, and those who move too slow are left behind.

Did you know?

To say, "I could care less," is to say it is possible to care more. The careless weed is called *bledo* in Spanish. In Guatemala, bledo is boiled, drained and chopped with onions, tomatoes and cilantro. It grows wild in the desert and, if necessary, can be eaten raw.

Did you know?

I learned about bledo from a Guatemalteca named Nancy. She could share more lessons with you than I ever could. Nancy has crossed twice, and when she talks about her daughter, Fatima, she cries.

Did you know?

Compañero is Spanish for willing to ask, willing to listen, willing to know.

PART IV

Letter from Home

Mommy,

Before I go to bed at night, I walk into the street to find a star to wish upon. I check my Minnie Mouse suitcase packed with new chonies and a bathing suit. "Ready for Florida," we said before you left, and I dream of the day you send for me. Till then, I promise to be brave like a bolt of blue lightning. Mommy, I promise to never stop dreaming.

Your Little Doll

Our Lady of the Water Gallons

Un mensaje a mis compañeros
Arivaca, AZ

I etch black line Sharpie Virgenes
on plastic water gallons: one arc,
Ichthys in the sand at travelers' feet;
one post carving, hobo's mark
on the road. The Virgen speaks to faceless
shadows traveling when the land is dark.
I etch black line Sharpie Virgenes

on plastic water gallons. One arc
is the bridge between L.A. and Arivaca,
liquor store murals and water drawings,
dogs on lawns and dogs trained to attack a
man and woman darting up Hippie Mountain.
They've hiked this far from Guatemala
on one plastic water gallon, one arc.

Ichthys in the sand at travelers' feet
is the tale of a man left shirtless and shoeless
beside thorny mesquite. Como un pez sin agua,
he is fished off the road limp and nearly witless.
In the arms of compañeros he asks,
"¿Es esto sentir la muerte?" Barely conscious

78

he is Ichthys in the sand at traveler's feet.

One post carving, hobo's mark,
would mark our "angel food" with a cross,
but cross signs feel wrong to fingers
wanting a symbol with less power, more loss,
like desert flower blooms, or a growing belly
beneath blue robes of water and gloss.
I need one post carving, hobo's mark.

On the road, the Virgen speaks to faceless
suffering. A woman seven months pregnant
hikes with garlic-lashed calves (snake safe-guard).
Bleeding and cramping, body bent
to ground, she makes mud salves and prayers
to Our Mother: *keep my unborn daughter radiant.*
On the road, the Virgen speaks. To faceless

shadows traveling when the land is dark,
I say, I see the fresh footprint in the riverbed,
the torn blanket ditched on the hillside.
At a rest stop shaded by oak, I tread
slow, count empty gallons, read what remains.
I promise you are not invisible, nor discarded,
people traveling when the land is dark.

I etch black line Sharpie Virgenes
to cloak rocky paths in stars
and hope one will guide you home.
When muscles spasm and farm lights appear too far,
know that I built this poem with safe spaces.
But because no words can erase your scars,
I etch black line Sharpie Virgenes.

Face Wipes for Sensitive Skin

Arivaca, AZ

We stand,
two stunned columns,
at the face of Daisy's tent.

She doles out a nightly ration,
one wet nap each,
pulled from blue plastic package.

I cherish this white square,
slowly wipe away
at day's sweat, dirt and ache

from forehead,
from under eyes,
from creases of my nose.

She wipes away
at day's sweat, dirt and ache

from forehead,
from under eyes,
from creases of her nose.

We rub circles.

Fingertips follow contours of bone,
linger along temples,
contemplate eye sockets.

We do not talk.

I ache to be clean,
to be soft,
to be touched.

I ache for relief
from brash suns burning.

"Are you O.K.?"

Rub circles.

"Did you hear the couple say whichever one makes it
will send for their daughter?"

Fingertips along bone.

"How can this be
my country?"

She washes her pinked peach skin.

"How can this be
my country?"

I wash my rosed caramel skin.

The sun begins to descend
below the hills of the Sonoran desert.

More circles. More bones.

Diana Shuts the Water to Listen

Torn, cotton underwear hang on tree branches
like fake gold trophies with fake swollen muscles,
like streamers pushed by winds into desert dances.

Diana bathes naked, tanned skin with splashes
from a farmhouse garden hose. Red water puddles.
Her soiled, cotton underwear hangs on tree branches.

Dark period trickles down her thighs. Memory flashes
charred trees and shredded skin of raw knuckles
like streamers pushed by winds into desert dances.

She temporarily forgets wailing ghosts in long grasses.
Ground water sooths cramps and images of shiny buckles
and torn, cotton underwear dangling from tree branches.

Diana's buzzed, blond hair shimmers and catches
the sun, but her button blue eyes gray with troubles
like streamers caught by winds in desert dances.

Diana shuts the water to listen beyond Arizona ranches
for muffled cries of women that everyday double
because torn, cotton underwear hang on tree branches
like streamers pushed by winds into desert dances.

The Ascension of Josseline

Two small, blistered
and bleeding feet dip
into one of the stone pools
pocking the ravine
like the face of the moon.
That orange moon being eaten
by the sun, eclipsed.
The sun is cruel
gulping what flamed tongues touch.
Since they lick nearly everything
nearly everything is licked,
including Josseline.

She removed one jacket,
before removing the second,
removed the right green shoe
before the left,
one sock before the next,
rolled up each leg of her
impossible-Hollywood-dream pants
and washed her feet
in sacred stone pools.
This is how she prepared
with ritual and prayer
and waited for her ascension.

If I Was John Diego, or A Border Patrol Officer's Poem

I am so thirsty, she choked.
Spotted her while on patrol curled up to a blooming cholla.
Thought she was dead,
but then she opened her eyes.
She must have been hallucinating
because she mistook me for the Mexican Mary.
Picked her up in my arms. Walked her to shade.
Fed her water from my canteen.
That's when she screamed, *Don't touch me!*
Lunged like a cat, *My earrings double as shanks!*
or maybe something about knives,
and passed out.

When I was a boy, my father taught me
how to spin a good story and to always say Yes, sir,
how to lead a momma and her ducklings to water,
how to keep the muzzle of my gun from touching the dirt,
but never how to bring a dying girl to life.

If I was that Indian boy, John Diego,
it would have been water, not roses.
You know, they believe the Virgin Mary
appeared to that boy,
and he gathered roses from her feet.
He was probably a fucking faggot anyway.

Only a faggot would take spring
when he could have asked for springs.
I might not know much, but I do know,
if I had been Diego,
that girl would have never been thirsty.

Search and Recovery

Volunteers will not be combing the woods
in single file at the edge of a peach town;

police will not be dragging the lake; neighbors will not
be questioned, nor family members interviewed;

no pencil sketches will be drawn, no time-stamped videos
aired; white candles will not be lit at midnight;

no posters will be made, nor stories printed;
regularly scheduled programing will not be interrupted.

This will not stop two women from scaling
the Atascosa mountains like specs of dust.

The wind and scrape of rocks beneath their feet
will be the only noise that joins their search

for a young man shot by his coyote
and discarded by a wash with cement blocks

and black kites cut loose from the sky,
or maybe black tires stripped from a truck.

It will be futile, but they will exhaust every unreliable detail
until landmarks turn hot and hazy. They will hike

with supplies slung over backs: extra water, socks,
electrolyte pills, a couple of apples, peanut butter.

At sunset, they will build camp beneath a pink sky,
close eyes with last light, open with first, and start again.

In the day, they will search for what remains.
In the night, they will fear what remains might look like.

Both will stay silent, too ashamed to say one hope aloud:
If we cross a bundle tomorrow, please let it be branches.

to chew   empty spaces

She craves conversation
to chew   empty spaces
where flash-images:
fleshy, gashed arms,
vacant, raisin eyes,
mounds beneath blankets,
(heartbeat to throat)
rise like   dead.

But Bernadette remains
relatively close-lipped
like   grandmother at Lent,
showing reverence for ghosts
that refuse to be swallowed.

"We sleep on cots
gathered in   open
because it's better than
being alone," she said.
"Because it's better."

I sleep in   one-person tent,

swat   foot of my sleeping bag,
listen for hisses and rattles,
but hear revs and calls
of 4-wheeled drug pickups
in   gulch below.
My thoughts circle
with helicopters over head.
I close eyes
to visualize   color blue,
    quench of water.

Yesterday, I walked Bernadette
to Byrd's ranch, carrots in hand,
to help her feed   horses.
I watched yellow bees drink
from troughs, listened to   buzzing.

Here is where she shared

    story of   girlfriend
abandoned in Brooklyn
along with   apartment,
    one broken into
while they were home
awake.
"She thinks I left her
for another woman," she said.

Bernadette is like that apartment.

She and I sit side-by-side
on   roof of   silver Silverado
and enjoy   sun's return over
    teeth of   jagged night.

This is my final morning.

We share   cigarette
note   flash of   storm
rumbling our way.
I think,   *desert is ocotillo*
calling   rain open-mouthed
with too many tongues,
but Bernadette already knows this,
and I say nothing

because it's better.

Letter from the Desert

To my daughter,

No regrets. No regrets. No regrets. No regrets. No regrets.
No regrets. No regrets. No regrets. No regrets. No regrets.
No regrets. No regrets. No regrets. No regrets. No regrets.
No regrets. No regrets. No regrets. No regrets. No regrets.
No regrets. No regrets. No regrets. No regrets. No regrets.
No regrets. No regrets. No regrets. No regrets. No regrets.
No regrets. No regrets. No regrets. No regrets. No regrets.
No regrets. No regrets. No regrets. No regrets. No regrets.

Just love.

Your mother

I Didn't Know I Could Love the Desert

Abiquiu, NM, June 2012

Maybe I always heard the desert calling my name
in the middle of the night keeping me up restless.
Maybe that's why I didn't know I could love;
I was grumpy from lack of sleep.
I didn't know I would want to hug the rounded cholla.
Cholla, if I could I would sew a felt and string teddy bear version of you
with stubby arms and purple flowers to hug at night.
You look so full and content.
I didn't know cactus could be content.
I didn't know cactus had more than one name: barrel, cholla,
nopal, saguaro. I have yet to write a poem for the saguaro!
The tall and proud saguaro honoring the sun with outstretched arms.
I love outstretched arms!
I love to dance with arms stretched out to the sky.
Arms feel light like that.
Sometimes I wish arms never had to come down.
I do not love the come down
and hangovers that demolish the brain
leaving trembles in the hands like after a bombing.
I shouldn't compare Sunday morning wrecks to world destruction,
but I can't help being a narcissist now and again.
The wind kicks up dust and little white bits of soft dream.
I want to float on one of those bits escaped

from the branches of a cottonwood.

I want to be a bit of white, soft nothing floating between junipers
at sunset, free to lift all the last bits of light.

In Arizona, there is nothing light and delicate.

But sometimes, in the middle of a heat-stroked day,
there can be laughter. I love laughter.

Nancy found a cross-color Rasta hat in a black trash bag
of donated clothes from well-meaning church ladies.

She put it on and did a little shimmy in Byrd Camp.

She momentarily forgot border patrol trucks patrolling the road
just outside our gate.

I momentarily forgot just being with Nancy was a crime.

And we both laughed— just a little.

I didn't know I could love Nancy.

Mesas are for New Mexico, and canyons are for Arizona.

Freeways are for L.A., and everything is covered by an epidermis of dust.

Dust on cars, dust on windows, dust on toes, dust in eyes,
dust filming white teeth. Dust sticks like guilt.

Somehow, I think I could love the dust too.

Nobody Wanted a Mountain to Hate Him

> If one man killed another in a battle
> he would quickly turn away
> from the man's sacred mountain
> before the mountain saw his face.
> —Byrd Baylor

If one man conquers another's land,
he quickly turns away from new borders
scratched in sand so as not to look
into the eyes of those he means to forget.

Nobody cares if he is hated, or maybe
it's better to say, it is impossible to be hated
by what no longer exists.
What was once sacred no longer exists.

I once climbed a sacred mountain and rested
at a pass known only as Dead Man's.
Dead Man should consider building a fence
around his pass if it is truly his and he means to keep it.

Nobody wants to be without
one free pass, especially a dead man.
Nobody battles and kills many things
he never learned how to hold.

The face of the mountain scowls at what
has happened to its land. The sheer granite
face of the mountain erodes, erasing
all emotion because it is tired of hating.

The sheer number of dead men is enough
to make any mountain turn its back.

Meditation for the Lost and Found

"You won't get lost if you take the road to the left and bear to the left at every crossroad."
    –Jorge Luis Borges

Baboquivari Peak is plastered on water gallons like children on milk cartons. If lost, keep Babo
Peak to your left to find your way north. If lost, expect bones to be found by scorpions. Babo is
an   "incase
of":   incase of forgetting, incase of getting left behind. But you have already run   dry and
drop   ped Babo on the ridge of _____ Man's Pass. Border Patrol ambushed your   group
with   semi-   auto   matic
rifles and   everyone has scattered. You are alone. You scramble to find   north, find the
lights of a   ranch house, find another person. You are safe in your Phoenix   home   with
your   child ren gathered   at your feet.   They   remove
your   shoes   and ask about   the layers of dry, scaled blist ers. You tell   them   their
father nearly became a   snake. You never see your   children a   gain.   You
never   got to   have a child,   but as you   lay your head   in the sand   and   close
your   eyes,   you hear her   easy laugh   echoing up   through the   Ata   scosas.
You   are   found in the   fetal position, a prayer card   of San Judas   crump   led in
your   fist.   You are found   by BP and   sent to deten   tion. The open   gash   on your
knee   goes   unexamined.   Your body   goes unbathed.   In a wood-   panel   ed and
beige   feder   al courtroom,   you sit next   to others like   you, pungent   and   petri
fied,   ankles and wrists   shackled one   pair to the   next. You   move   before
the   judge   in unison,   chains jingling like Christ   mas, and you   feel   like a
rein   deer,   like a snow   dog, like an   animal. You   never see a   judge. You are
drag   ged to the border   south of San   Diego and   are   beaten
and   tased   five times. You never again set foot on Mexi   can soil, but   your   screams
for   help   are heard on both sides of the wall. You walk   in the dark   and   carry a
back   pack   stuffed with   drugs. You
carry   this backpack because if you don't, the man with a gun pointed at   your   house
will   open fire. Because if you don't, the man with the gun pointed at your   house   will
step   inside and
find your sister. Because if you don't, she has no chance. You have no choice. There are   no
drugs. You walk for work for a safe place, for a kiss from your wife and to be lost in   the
                                                                                             scent of
her hair. Your legs are cramping. You no longer know why Babo is important. You have lost the
meaning of water. You are lost. You are *desaparecido*, which means, you will never be found.

The Boys of Summer

Carpinteria, CA, July 2014

In Carpinteria, California a golden preteen in red shorts
runs down a clouded over beach to play at junior lifeguard.
He is lost in a sea of boys and girls just like him
all smiling and learning lessons on how to be safe.

In Brooks County, Texas a boy with a note pinned to his shirt
addressed to an aunt in New Jersey wrestles
with his mother's hopes pinned to his shoulders.
Dehydration pins his cramping leg muscles together.

On a beach in Gaza four cousins play soccer.
One calls Messi while another calls Neymar before the injury.
The score is tied. They set up penalty kicks on the edge
of the surf. A boat in the distance sets up its shot.

The boy digs toes into sand and waits for his turn
to relay to a solo buoy bouncing in the water.
He asks the cute and sunny blond in line next to him,
"If you could live anywhere, where would you live?"

Alone in the desert, the boy lies down in the dirt.
As he closes his eyes he dreams of the home he is to build
for his mother and sister where he will watch all the TV

he wants, and no one worries about being killed.

On a beach in Gaza the four boys are blown to Jello-y pieces
of matter, and now they'll never know a life without fear.
The mothers and fathers gather outside the hospital and scream
into the air because they couldn't give their boys a safe place to play.

Ventana

After Javier Sicilia
Los Angeles, CA

At the Alvarado off ramp, a gray bearded god conjures storms of pigeons
with seeds spat from cracked and drooling lips.
In San Gabriel, my father insists I cease being angry.
My brother imagines blowing his brains out.
"My boss said, You look like you could slash your own throat."
You look like you will slash your own throat.
Empty houses spread throughout Los Angeles and metastasize
into abysses of treachery, dens of abuse.
A young girl (more than one and more than once) is raped
on a stained and discarded mattress. Lying on her back
she can see a forgotten cross hanging above her head.
Jesus has forgotten to mobilize.
Black spray paint explains, Jesus ya no vive aquí.
In DF, Mexico, a poet decorated with medallions like a saint
challenges a properly suited president in a great hall,
"You didn't steal my wife, but you did kill my son."
The son shot dead and swept out of the street like trash.
The son piled up with thousands of other dead sons
and daughters in a stinking heap.
A friend (I will not name) hung himself in his bedroom.
I was in the desert at the time without phone service.
I remember him grooving, shirt open, on the dance floor. Now I fear

phone service in the desert.
I fear whatever makes a woman's scream shatter a moonless Arizona frontier—
hair-raising wounded cries of a woman made out to be a beast,
guttural gritos with the power to shift time and space.
My world has shifted.
This world is a carcass being picked at by scavengers.
I want to scream, I AM angry! I am fucking angry!
The dude that stood me up more than once calls me
in the middle of the night for a fuck.
Something about a hard cock a cat couldn't scratch makes me not want to scratch.
I want this poem to not be true.
I want to wrestle each member of my family to the ground one by one.
I want the desert to be magical.
I want four tires running over Route 66 to reclaim lost things.
I want an opulent sunrise over mounds of Technicolored red-rocked Sedona.
In Arizona, a young man is found off Chavez Road
so close to death volunteers say they convened with his spirit.
I am in Byrd Camp when we get the call
nursing a woman with critical kidneys and a sprained ankle.
"Si no lo encontraron," she says. "Si fuera una noche mas. Si fuera."
I touch my hand to her shoulder. Tears flood our eyes.
I touch one hand to her shoulder and an electric burning fuses us as one.
Cut off the hand. Cut away all this impossible feeling.
In L.A., I walk Radio Hill and track trickling dirt trails just like Arizona.
Barbed wire fences have cut openings. Nopales take up residence on slopes.
A mattress lays nestled in tall grass, and I catch a glimpse of an elderly man
hobbling into the bush out of sight.

I hope to live to see a time when mattresses return to bedrooms
and bedrooms are allowed to once again house dreams.
The windows of all the houses have been muddied or boarded up.
I can't see a god, but I want one.

The Poem I'm Writing Already Wonders About Its Worth

After Eloise Klein Healy

Sometimes my niece and nephew
stay the night, and in the mornings
I tie a red apron around my waist
and flip fluffy omelets onto their plates.
They smile as they chew.
Sometimes I place a hand over round, little heads
and pretend they are mine.

Most nights, I lurk alone in bars
or dating sites looking for one person
to kiss, to hold, to invite into my bed
and feel his belly pressed up to my back,
my body cradled in his,
making the world warm and quiet
enough to sleep.

The poem I am writing is not about borders.
The poem I am writing is not about death.

Or the miracle of spotting a man stashed
on a dusty, nameless hill when none of his comrades
could finish the job of strangling him.

God willing (he might say), *I will return*
to my farm and my wife and my children,
and they will hold me so tight
I'll remember what it is to breathe.

This poem wonders what it would be like
to cook breakfast on a Saturday morning
for a man still lying in bed,
for babies still fast asleep,
to know what it is to have something
worth dying for, to have a home
worth living for when the world has gone dark.

Nancy's Story, or the Words I Want to Get Right

I know the pond where you and the others went swimming. The helicopter swooped down on our group. Everyone scattered, but Francisco and I ran together for a mountain. The helicopter's spotlight swept the floor behind us.

They released the dogs. It was dark, but we ran. Cactus needles, rattlesnakes, the edge of a cliff. We didn't know what was in front of us. My hair got caught in the thorns of a tree. Look here, you can see the tree kept half.

My arms are cut and bruised. You have cuts too, but you walk during the day. You follow a trail, and there are no dogs.

In pitch-black we found Hippie Mountain and the pond. Once the dogs and helicopters were gone, we climbed down and walked around the water. We looked, but we found no one. We walked for two days without food or water.

I crossed once before, but it was different. I was seven months pregnant. Half way through, I started cramping. I covered my belly in mud. I prayed to the Virgin Mother.

This time my knees buckled. I choked. I cried, "We're going to die out here! We're going to die!" like a crazy woman. Francisco grabbed me and shook me until I stopped.

He walked me to a hilltop and pointed to the distance, "Do you see those houses?" I saw dots of light and nodded.

"We will to go those houses, knock on those doors, and someone will help us." Then we climbed back down. The lights disappeared, and I started to cry all over again.

When we couldn't walk anymore, we lied down in the dirt. I pictured my daughter, Fatima, waiting to meet us in Florida, but this time I didn't cry.

Then we noticed a green light above our heads. "What's that?" I asked. "I don't know," Francisco said, and we followed it here. Your friend came out of the darkness. Before I could be scared he said, "We're friends here. You're safe."

"You're safe here," he said, and I dropped to my knees and screamed.

A NOTE ON DESERT POEMS

In August 2011, I volunteered as a desert aid worker in the "Tucson Sector" of the Mexico-U.S. border with the direct humanitarian aid organization, No More Deaths. All summer the organization accepts volunteers to camp and hike the militarized, low-grade warzone known as our borderlands in order to patrol migrant trails, replenish water and food supplies, act as witness to Border Patrol abuses, and assist in their mission to end the death and suffering of individuals crossing the desert in order to find work, family members, and safety.

According to U.S. Customs and Border Protection there were 363 deaths on the southwest border in the 2011 fiscal year. This does not include unrecovered remains or missing persons.

As a daughter of Mexican immigrants, an Angeleno and a poet, I have always been interested in immigration stories and reform. When I volunteered with NMD, I wanted to do something off the page and physical to help, and I hoped that by standing on the desert sand, watching the helicopters circle, feeling my skin burn under the sun, I might be able to turn the abstract border and "wall" into something more tangible for those back in California and beyond. This was the inspiration for the desert poems in PART III and IV.

For more information on No More Deaths or how to volunteer, you can visit: www.nomoredeaths.org.

THANK YOU

Thank you to *Poets & Writers* and Marilyn Chin for selecting a portion of this collection as the winning poetry manuscript of the 2013 California Writers Exchange and to Tucson Festival of Books and Denise Chávez for selecting poems from this collection for third place in the 2015 literary awards.

I would like to acknowledge the poets that made this collection possible by sharing their time and words with me through emails, readings, workshops, meet-ups, and Skype dates namely Erika Ayon, Molly Bendall, Nikia Chaney, Lisa Cheby, Maya Chinchilla, Jenny Factor, Jamie Asaye Fitzgerald, Jerry Garcia, Marisa Urrutia Gedney, Liz Gonzalez, Sonia Guiñansaca, Lisa McCool-Grime, Scott Miller, Marilyn Nelson, Christine Castro Ruiz, Yaccaira Salvatierra, and Allison Tobey.

I send thanks to Angél García, Kenji Liu and Terry Wolverton for their invaluable notes on the full manuscript, and to Eduardo C. Corral and Verónica Reyes for their advice.

To Olga García Echeverría, Melinda Palacio, Jesús Salvador Treviño, Micheal Sedano and *La Bloga* for their kind support.

To Cristina García for creating Las Dos Brujas Writers' Workshop, a five-day experience that leaves its impression on this collection. To Juan Felipe Herrera and the Adobe Dojo poets for bringing joy and experimentation to my poetry. To Ashaki M. Jackson and Ramona Pilar for sharing the drive to Ghost Ranch, New Mexico and for their friendship.

To the Citrons—Melissa Chadburn, Antonia Crane, Trish Falin, Seth Fischer, Rachel Kann, Matthew McDonald, Tina Rubin, Diane Sherlock, Judy Sunderland, and Sakena

Washington—for giving me the strength to keep believing in and fighting for this book. To Kate Maruyama for being a soundboard in a difficult decision. And to Tisha Reichle for her willingness to show up for all of us time and time again and for making our community bright.

To all the women of Women Who Submit, and its creator Alyss Dixson, for being the most down literary girl gang ever with shout outs to Lauren Eggert-Crowe, Ashley Perez, Rachael Warecki and Laura Warrell.

I thank Erin Elizabeth Smith and everyone at Sundress Publications for giving this collection a home when I was most worried it wouldn't find one.

I send special thanks to Eloise Klein Healy for challenging me to write from a more personal place, and though I never had a chance to meet her, to Michele Serros for being my Chicana role model.

This manuscript would have never found its direction if it wasn't for No More Deaths. I would like to thank all the volunteers who welcomed and helped me during my time on the border and to thank those volunteers that continue to work year-round to end suffering in the desert. I thank "Nancy" for sharing her stories with me and for teaching me about human suffering and kindness.

The deepest appreciation goes to my family—Julio Bermejo, Gabriel Bermejo, Enid Bermejo, Andrés-David Bermejo, Raquel Cagigas, Gabrielito Bermejo, Armando Cagigas-Bermejo, Paola Bermejo, and Aurora Cagigas-Bermejo—for loving and inspiring me everyday. And to Dorothy Dubois, Barbara Anne Dubois, and all the Duboises for making our family three times bigger. I also want to thank Ermelinda Bermejo for buying me my first journal, Analisa DeHaro for never doubting I was a writer, and Alma Rosa Bermejo Medrano for always believing this book would be published. To Alia Vajrabukka and Christina Thornell for being cheerleaders and gentle first readers when I needed it, and to Teresa Santilena, Justin Blackburn, and Jay Myers for keeping me sane and laughing.

Finally, I thank my mom and dad, Imelda and Ruben Bermejo, for teaching me about hard work, bravery, and compassion, for encouraging me to follow my dreams and to put my name on it. I am an artist because of them.

ABOUT THE AUTHOR

Xochitl-Julisa Bermejo is a first generation Chicana born and raised in San Gabriel, California, who fondly remembers weekends spent haciendo traviesos with her cousins around her grandparents' Boyle Heights home. She wrote this collection while living in a house in the shadows of Dodger Stadium in historic Solano Canyon.

Bermejo is a 2016-2017 Steinbeck fellow and was previously honored as a *Poets & Writers* California Writers Exchange poetry winner, Barbara Deming Memorial Fund/Money for Women grantee, Los Angeles Central Library ALOUD newer poet, and her poetry received 3rd place in the 2015 Tucson Festival of Books literary awards. She has received residencies with Hedgebrook, the Ragdale Foundation, and is a proud member of the Macondo Writers' Workshop.

In Los Angeles, she is a cofounder of Women Who Submit, a literary organization using social media and community events to empower women authors to submit work for publication, and curates the quarterly reading series HITCHED. She received a BA in Theatre Arts from California State University of Long Beach and an MFA in Creative Writing from Antioch University Los Angeles where she is currently a book coach and workshop instructor with the inspiration2publication program.

OTHER SUNDRESS TITLES

Theater of Parts
M. Mack
$15

Every Love Story is an Apocalypse Story
Donna Vorreyer
$14

Ha Ha Ha Thump
Amorak Huey
$14

major characters in minor films
Kristy Bowen
$14

Hallelujah for the Ghosties
Melanie Jordan
$14

When I Wake It Will Be Forever
Virginia Smith Rice
$14

Suites for the Modern Dancer
Jill Khoury
$15

What Will Keep Us Alive
Kristin LaTour
$14

Stationed Near the Gateway
Margaret Bashaar
$14

Confluence
Sandra Marchetti
$14

Fortress
Kristina Marie Darling
$14

A House of Many Windows
Donna Vorreyer
$14

CPSIA information can be obtained
at www.ICGtesting.com
Printed in the USA
LVHW061235040622
720412LV00033B/283